W9-AMP-310

Color in My World

Red Around Me

Madeline Stevens

Cavendish Square
New York

Published in 2015 by Cavendish Square Publishing, LLC
243 5th Avenue, Suite 136, New York, NY 10016

Library of Congress Cataloging-in-Publication Data

Stevens, Madeline, author.
Red around me / Madeline Stevens.
pages cm. — (Color in my world)
Includes index.
ISBN 978-1-50260-060-8 (hardcover) ISBN 978-1-50260-059-2 (paperback) ISBN 978-1-50260-061-5 (ebook)
1. Red—Juvenile literature. 2. Colors—Juvenile literature. 3. Color—Juvenile literature. I. Title.

QC495.5.S7487 2015
535.6—dc23

2014024960

Editor: Andrew Coddington
Senior Copy Editor: Wendy A. Reynolds
Art Director: Jeffrey Talbot
Designer: Joseph Macri
Senior Production Manager: Jennifer Ryder-Talbot
Production Editor: David McNamara
Photo Research by J8 Media

The photographs in this book are used by permission and through the courtesy of: Cover photo, Alan Majchrowicz/The Image Bank/Getty Images; Tatiana Grozetskaya/Shutterstock.com, 5; Hugh Adams/Shutterstock.com, 7; James Steidl/Shutterstock.com, 9; eabff/iStock/Thinkstock, 11; Karaidel/iStock/Thinkstock, 13; Kseniia Perminova/Shutterstock.com, 15; StevenRussellSmithPhotos/Shutterstock.com, 17; Henrik_L/iStock/Thinkstock, 19; Natursports/Shutterstock.com, 21.

Printed in the United States of America

Contents

The color red is all around us.

In fall, some leaves on trees turn bright red.

4

5

These red apples have just been picked.

They are **crisp** and **delicious** to eat.

This fire truck is painted red.

It **warns** us to be **careful** when the truck races to a fire.

8

9

Stop signs are red.

They tell drivers when to stop and wait until it is safe to drive.

11

We celebrate Valentine's Day with red hearts.

They tell people we love them.

13

People give red roses to those they love.

Roses are very **beautiful**.

14

15

Many animals and birds
are red.

A cardinal's red feathers make
it stand out.

17

Some very small **insects** are red.

This ladybug is munching on a leaf.

19

This red sports car can drive fast.

Red is an exciting color!

New Words

beautiful (BYOO-ti-ful) Pretty to look at.

careful (KARE-ful) Watch out for danger.

crisp (KRISP) Fresh and firm.

delicious (de-LIH-shus) Tasty.

insects (IN-sekts) Small animals that often have six legs and wings.

warns (WORNS) To tell someone of a possible danger.

Index

23

About the Author

Madeline Stevens is a writer and former teacher. She lives in New York with her husband, son, and dog, Roxy.

About

Bookworms help independent readers gain reading confidence through high-frequency words, simple sentences, and strong picture/text support. Each book explores a concept that helps children relate what they read to the world they live in.